Paper Mosaics
in an afternoon®

Paper Mosaics
in an afternoon®

Marie Browning

Sterling Publishing Co., Inc.
New York

Prolific Impressions Production Staff:

Editor in Chief: Mickey Baskett
Copy Editor: Phyllis Mueller
Graphics: Lampe-Farley Communications
Styling: Lenos Key, Marie Browning
Photography: Jerry Mucklow Rocket Photography, Visions West Photography
Administration: Jim Baskett

Library of Congress Cataloging-in-Publication Data Available

10 9 8 7 6 5 4 3 2 1

Published by Sterling Publishing Co., Inc.
387 Park Avenue South, New York, N.Y. 10016
©2006 by Prolific Impressions, Inc.
Produced by Prolific Impressions, Inc.
160 South Candler St., Decatur, GA 30030

Distributed in Canada by Sterling Publishing
c/o Canadian Manda Group, 165 Dufferin St.,
Toronto, Ontario, Canada M6K 3H6
Distributed in the United Kingdom by GMC Distribution Services,
Castle Place, 166 High Street, Lewes, East Sussex, England BN7 1XU
Distributed in Australia by Capricorn Link (Australia) Pty. Ltd.
P.O. Box 704, Windsor, NSW 2756, Australia

Printed in China
All rights reserved

Sterling ISBN-13: 978-1-4027-2443-5
         ISBN-10: 1-4027-2443-8

For information about custom editions, special sales, premium and corporate purchases, please contact Sterling Special Sales Department at 800-805-5489 or specialsales@sterlingpub.com

Acknowledgements

I thank these manufacturers for their generous contributions of quality products and support in the creation of the projects in this book:

For decoupage papers from Australia and Scrap Art:
Artifacts, Inc.
Palestine, Texas, USA
www.artifactsinc.com

For acrylic paints and texture paint:
Delta Technical Coatings
Whittier, California, USA
www.deltacrafts.com

For two-part polymer resin coating (Envirotex-Lite), plastic measuring cups, disposable brushes, stir sticks, and thin-bodied glue (Ultra-Seal):
Environmental Technology, Inc.
Fields Landing, California, USA
www.eti-usa.com

For cutting tools:
Fiskars Brands, Inc.
Wausau, Wisconsin, USA
www.fiskars.com

For artist canvas board:
Fredrix
Lawrenceville, Georgia, USA
www.fredrixartistcanvas.com

For decorative papers and scrapbook embellishments and stickers:
K & Company
Parkville, Missouri, USA
www.kandcompany.com

For paint brushes and sponges:
Loew-Cornell Inc.
www.loew-cornell.com

For acrylic paints, decoupage mediums, decoupage prints, acrylic varnishes, dimensional varnish;
Plaid Enterprises, Inc.
Norcross, Georgia, USA
www.plaidonline.com

For Italian Soft-Paper Decoupage Papers and decoupage mediums:
To-Do Designs
Italy
www.to-do.it

For wooden surfaces:
Stone Bridge Collection
Ontario, Canada
www.stonebridgecollection.com

For wooden surfaces and the Versa Tool Heat Cutter:
Walnut Hollow
Dodgeville, Wisconsin, USA
www.walnuthollow.com

About Marie Browning

A consummate craft designer, Marie Browning has made a career of designing products, writing books and articles, and teaching and demonstrating. You may have been charmed by her creative acumen but not been aware of the woman behind it; she has designed stencils, stamps, transfers, and a variety of other award-winning product lines for art and craft supply companies. As well as writing numerous books on creative living, Marie's articles and designs have appeared in numerous home decor and crafts magazines.

Marie Browning earned a Fine Arts Diploma from Camosun College and attended the University of Victoria. She is a Certified Professional Demonstrator, a design member of the Crafts and Hobby Association (CHA), and a board member of the Society of Craft Designers (SCD). Marie also serves on the committee for SCD that researches and writes about upcoming trends in the arts and crafts industry. In 2004 she was selected by *Craftrends* trade publication as a Top Influential Industry Designer.

She lives, gardens, and crafts on Vancouver Island in Canada. She and her husband Scott have three children: Katelyn, Lena, and Jonathan. Marie can be contacted at www.mariebrowning.com

Other Books by Marie Browning Published by Sterling
Snazzy Jars (2006)
Jazzy Gift Baskets (2005)
Purse Pizzazz (2005)
Really Jazzy Jars (2005)
Totally Cool Polymer Clay for Kids (2005)
Totally Cool Soapmaking for Kids (2004, reprinted in softcover)
Wonderful Wraps (2003, reprinted in softcover)
Jazzy Jars (2003, reprinted in softcover)
Designer Soapmaking (2003, reprinted in German)
300 Recipes for Soap (2002, reprinted in softcover and in French)
Crafting with Vellum and Parchment (2001, reprinted in softcover with the title *New Paper Crafts*)
Melt & Pour Soapmaking (2000, reprinted in softcover)
Hand Decorating Paper (2000, reprinted in softcover)
Memory Gifts (2000, reprinted in softcover with the title *Family Photocrafts*)
Making Glorious Gifts from Your Garden (1999, reprinted in softcover)
Handcrafted Journals, Albums, Scrapbooks & More (1999, reprinted in softcover)
Beautiful Handmade Natural Soaps (1998, reprinted in softcover with the title *Natural Soapmaking*)

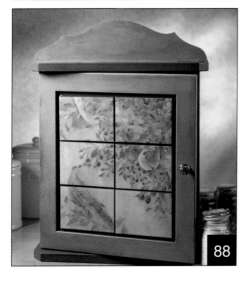

PAPER MOSAICS *in an afternoon*®

Simple, Beautiful Mosaics with Paper

A mosaic, by definition, is a picture or decorative design made by setting small colored pieces such as stones or tiles on a surface. Throughout history, mosaics have been created with everything from pebbles, glass, and precious metals to terra cotta shards, ceramic tiles, and found materials. This book explores new mosaic techniques that use a variety of decorative papers to create the mosaic look with supplies and equipment that are readily obtainable and inexpensive.

Using papers for designing mosaic pieces allows you to enjoy the mosaic art form without the labor of cutting tiles, the expense of traditional materials, or the mess of grouting. Using basic crafts materials and a few simple tools, pieces of beautifully colored and decorated papers are cut and glued to surfaces to create the magnificent look of mosaics.

Paper mosaic techniques are basically decoupage techniques, but for paper mosaics, the paper pieces are cut into mosaic shapes and glued with spaces between the pieces to imitate the look of grout lines. You can use decoupage paper, decorative scrapbooking papers,

self-adhesive stickers, images from magazines, wrapping paper, and color photocopies to make paper mosaics projects, including tables, boxes, trays, and wall pieces, that you will be proud to display and give as gifts. What else could you cover? The possibilities are endless, and artistic skills are not required.

This book includes everything you need to get started—detailed information on supplies and tools and instructions for the basic techniques used to create the projects. There are numerous photographs and step-by-step instructions for more than 40 projects to guide and inspire you. Enjoy!

History of Mosaics

While developing the techniques for this book, I found learning about the history of mosaics a valuable and interesting exercise. The word "mosaic" comes from the Greek and means "patient work, worthy of the Muses."

Mosaics have a rich, long history, dating back almost 4,000 years when terra cotta cones were pushed point first into a mud base to form a protective and decorative surface. By the 4th century B.C.E., pebbles of different colors were being used to create detailed geometric and pictorial scenes. The Greeks and Romans cut natural stone into small squares, rectangles, and triangles called *tesserae.* to create mosaics with more details and in a wider range of colors than could be accomplished with found stones. The mosaics unearthed at Pompeii illustrate this technique. (Today, the word tesserae is used to describe all the materials used to make mosaics.) Early Christian mosaics used glass tesserae.

The highest expression of the mosaic art form came during the Byzantine era (5th to 15th centuries, C.E.), when glass pieces--often backed with gold leaf--were used to cover entire walls and ceilings; because they weren't grouted, reflected light made the entire composition sparkle. When developing paper mosaic techniques, I used colored tissue paper for a glass-like tesserae effect.

Found objects were used in Victorian mosaic pieces called "putty pots" and "memory ware." Broken china pieces, buttons, small toys and other everyday objects were arranged on posts, jugs, or plates and the spaces were filled with linseed putty. Modern works include the stunning ceramic mosaics in Barcelona, Spain created in the early part of the 20th century by Antonio Gaudi. Gaudi's Guell Park incorporates broken ceramic dishes and other found objects, a revolutionary idea at the time in formal art and architecture.

The modern term for mosaics made with found objects is *pique assiette*, named after Raymonde Isidore of northern France who, between 1938 and 1964, created *La Maison Picassiette*, a house covered with broken crockery—plates, dishes, cups, and tiles. (An approximate English translation of *picassiette* is "scrounger" or "stealer of plates," but it is also supposedly a play on the words "Picasso of plates.")

Modern mosaic artists often use computer technology to design mosaic patterns that are detailed and precise.

Papers to Use

Decorative papers are available in a huge assortment of colors, designs, and textures. In just one walk around a scrapbooking, crafts, or art supply store, you will discover many papers to inspire you. Many different types of decorative papers can be used for paper mosaics, including thin **decoupage papers, tissue papers, handmade papers, card stock, and memory papers.**

Art Prints

Prints on heavier papers are easy to glue without wrinkling or creasing and can be coated successfully. Calendars and greeting cards offer an economical source for art prints.

Decoupage Papers

These types of papers provide an almost endless variety of beautiful papers. Decoupage papers from Australia and Italy are the finest available and offer a wide range of classic and beautiful motifs.

Memory Papers

The types of papers sold for scrapbook backgrounds and design elements are fine to use. These papers, available in the memory crafting departments of craft stores, offer coordinated papers that work well for Paper Shard Mosaics and Photo Display Tile Art techniques. Also look for **printed verses and stickers** to use as embellishments and accents.

Photographs & Ephemera

Photographs and both old and reproduction ephemera make interesting design elements for paper mosaics. Whole books of one-sided pages of re-printed ephemera can be found at crafts and scrapbooking stores, ready to cut and use. You can find old prints in secondhand or antiques stores or raid your (or your parents' or grandparents') attic for handwritten letters, postcards, and family records like birth and marriage certificates. You might also use pages from old books, old legal documents, and everyday items like tickets, labels, and certificates. TIP: Always photocopy valuable pieces rather than using the originals in your project.

Miscellaneous

Lightweight origami papers, napkins, tissue paper, and gift wrap are all good choices for paper mosaic projects.

Wood Veneer

These thin pieces of wood, available at hardware and craft stores, are used to make the faux wood inlay projects. *Option:* Use decorative paper printed with a wood design for an easy to cut and punch alternative.

Pictured:
1. Decoupage paper
2. Memory papers
3. Art prints
4. Calendar of art prints
5. Ephemera reproductions
6. Wood veneer

Cutting Tools & Techniques

The proper cutting tools are important for successful paper mosaic projects. When your tools are sharp, easy to handle, and job specific, creating a project is easy and stress free.

Paper Trimmer

When you wish to cut perfect squares or rectangles for "tiles", use a paper trimmer for cutting the decorative papers accurately and easily. I prefer the slide type of trimmer that is readily available at craft and art stores. A paper trimmer is also useful for cutting pieces of paper into narrow strips for accents and borders. For photo mosaics, I prefer to use the paper trimmer for perfectly cut pieces rather than to cut them by hand.

Art or Craft Knife

A good art or craft knife is essential for cutting foam core board and large art prints that do not fit in a paper trimmer. For most cutting jobs, a round-handled knife with a #11 blade works best. I prefer to use a heavy-duty art knife for cutting foam core tiles; the sturdy, larger blade is best for thicker (1/2") foam core board.

Tips for Successful Cutting with an Art Knife:

- Use a new blade, and change blades frequently for best results.
- A **metal ruler** with cork backing is the best straight edge to use when cutting with an art knife. The cork backing prevents slipping, and the knife blade can't cut the metal (like it can wood or plastic).
- Always use an art knife on a **cutting mat**. It prevents you from marring your work surface and the grid on the mat helps you cut perfectly square tiles. I prefer a mat with 1/4" markings.

Heat Cutter

This tool, with its heated cutting blade, makes it easy to cut through foam core board. It is especially recommended for beginners and helps avoid hand fatigue when cutting many tiles.

A heat cutter is recommended for the Tile Art technique of cutting shaped and curved foam core tiles. It's difficult to cut them with an art knife, but the heated blade cuts foam core easily and smoothly.

Scissors

For rough trimming prints and for hand cutting irregularly shaped mosaic pieces, I like to have both large and small blade scissors handy.

Decorative Punches

You can create detailed tiles using the many different decorative punches available. I especially like decorative corner punches.

Pictured:
1. Paper trimmer
2. Art knife
3. Blades for knife
4. Decorative punches
5. Large blade scissors
6. Small blade scissors
7. Ruler
8. Cutting mat
9. Heavy duty cutting knife
10. Heat cutter

Mosaic Cutting Techniques

The size of the paper pieces you cut should be project appropriate—that is, cut larger paper pieces for large projects and smaller pieces for small projects. Remember the smaller the paper mosaic pieces, the longer it takes to glue them in place and the more visually busy the composition will be.

In the following examples, I've used the same image as a sample to illustrate the different mosaic cutting techniques.

Method 1

Irregular shapes cut by hand for a random mosaic, for a geometric pattern, or to create an image.

Use a paper trimmer to cut a strip of paper, then cut the strips into smaller pieces with scissors. You can cut squares or rectangles or cut angled or three- or five-sided pieces. You can cut all the pieces at once since they won't be glued in order. Don't cut too many curved edges; they are harder to place in the composition and don't look traditional.

Method 2

Irregular shapes cut by hand for gluing in order.

Cut a strip from the image, then cut the mosaic pieces. After you cut a mosaic piece, glue it in place. I like to apply a thin layer of glue (no larger than 3" square) and place the pieces in that area--that way, I have time to slightly adjust the pieces, and it is quicker than applying glue for each and every piece. Gluing the pieces in order preserves the original image. TIP: Don't try to cut all the pieces and then glue them down. All it takes is a slight breeze from an open door to mix up your pieces.

Method 3

Cutting out shapes, then pieces.

This method is best for keeping images visually intact and imitates the Greek mosaic method that used small tesserae. Cut out the shapes of the design, then cut the shapes, one shape at a time, into mosaic pieces. Again, glue each piece as you go to avoid losing your place or mixing up the pieces. To keep images recognizable, avoid cutting through faces.

Tile Art Cutting Technique

Tile Art uses a print cut into pieces for the mosaic effect. If you are hesitant about cutting your print and fear making a mistake, practice your cuts on a piece of paper the same size as your print so you can feel more confident when cutting the actual print. The techniques below will help you identify the focal point (the part of the composition to which you wish to draw the viewer's eye) and avoid cutting through important features, e.g., faces. Use a paper trimmer for small prints and an art knife, cutting mat, and metal ruler for larger prints.

Step 1. Trim the print

First, trim the print to the same size as your surface. Next, trim off an amount that represents the grout lines between each tile. For example, if the surface is 8" x 8" and you plan to make nine tiles, remove 1" (two 1/4" grout lines plus 1/4" on each edge), for a trimmed size of 7" x 7". (I always make the grout lines 1/4" wide, but I vary the edge space depending on the surface and whether or not I'm creating a piece I plan to place in a frame.)

Step 2. Determine the focal point and make vertical cuts

Study the print to determine the focal point—the part of the composition to which you wish to draw the viewer's eye. Cut the print into vertical strips, taking care not to cut through important features such as faces. The strips don't have to be the same width—use the images in the print as guides.

Step 3. Cut strips into tiles

Cut each strip separately. The tiles need not be the same size—size is determined by the images in the print.

Punched Paper Medallions

Many decorative papers can be cut with handheld punches or corner and border punches. For folded-and-punched techniques, use a thin paper such as Origami paper. Thin papers can be folded and punched through multiple layers, yielding creative results other papers don't offer. This punched medallion technique can be used for mosaic card designs or for Byzantine-inspired projects. The example uses a fleur de lis corner hole punch.

1. Cut a 2" square of origami paper with a paper trimmer.
2. Fold the paper in half, then in half again to form a 1" square.
3. Punch all four corners of the folded square with a corner hole punch.
4. Unfold the paper to reveal the medallion.

Cutting Out Motifs

Follow these steps to cut out motifs.

1. Trim away excess paper around the motif using scissors.
2. Use an art knife and a cutting mat to cut out inside areas.
3. Use small, sharp, pointed scissors to cut away the paper from the outer edge of design. Hold the scissors at a 45-degree angle to cut the paper with a tiny beveled edge--this helps the motif to adhere snugly against the surface. Move the paper, not the scissors as you cut.

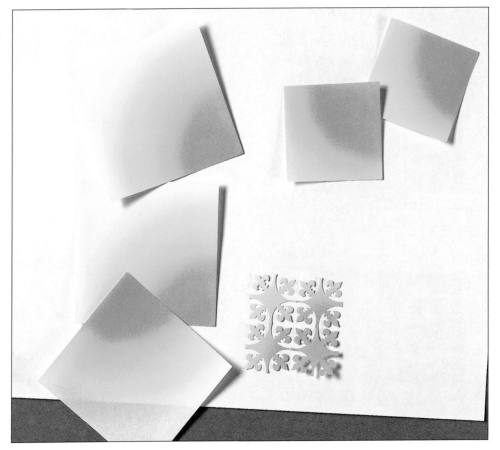

Surfaces

In the projects, the decorative papers are glued directly on prepared surfaces and on different thicknesses of foam. All the surfaces can be found at crafts, art supply, and home decorating outlets.

Thin Craft Foam

Used for the Paper Shard Mosaic technique, thin craft foam is readily available in craft stores, usually in the children's craft area. It comes in a variety of basic colors and is very easy to cut into small, intricate shapes. The foam also can be painted prior to covering with a translucent paper for greater color depth.

Foam Core Board

Foam core board cuts easily to create the tiles for the Tile Art technique—you can create tiles in various sizes and shapes for a variety of surfaces. Most projects use 3/16" thick white board; 3/16" black board and 1/2" thick board are also used.

Artist Canvas Boards

For Tile Art wall decor, artist canvas boards provide a firm, flat surface to which foam core tiles will adhere. Available at crafts and art supply stores, canvas boards come in sizes that fit standard frames, from 8" x 10" to 24" x 26". Archival canvas boards offer a rigid, non-warping hardboard core for larger Tile Art projects.

Wooden Surfaces

Unfinished wooden frames, boxes, trays, table tops, plaques, and plates are also great surfaces for paper mosaics. Decorative painting stores and crafts stores offer a wide selection of suitable unfinished wood pieces. I prefer wooden plates and platters over ceramic or glass pieces because the wooden surfaces are easier to paint and glue on and it's easy to attach a hanger. After a two-part polymer resin coating is applied, it's hard to tell the difference between a ceramic and a wooden piece.

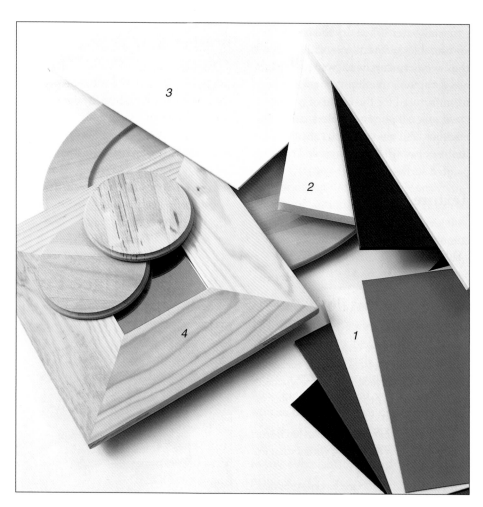

Pictured:
1. Thin craft foam
2. Foam core boards
    1/2" white
    3/16" black
    3/16" white
3. Artist canvas board
4. Wooden frame, plaques, platter

Glues

Decoupage medium

Use podge-type decoupage mediums to attach the paper pieces to your prepared surface. Podge-type mediums come in gloss, satin, and matte sheens as well as sepia tones and pearl finishes. (You can also use thin-bodied white glue to attach paper pieces—read on.)

Thin White Glue

Thin-bodied white glue goes on white and dries crystal clear. I use this glue for adhering foam core tiles and gluing paper pieces in the Tile Art technique and for sealing paper surfaces before applying a two-part polymer coating. (Thin-bodied white glue contains latex, which seals the paper pieces and prevents the resin coating from ruining the print.)

For sealing, two thin coats of glue are better than one heavy coat. Make sure the first coat is dry before brushing on a second coat, and let the second coat dry completely (it will be clear) before applying the resin coating. If the glue is just a little bit damp, it will turn white under the coating and ruin the design. **Do not** use a decoupage medium for the seal coat—it works great for adhering paper pieces but does not contain enough latex to seal the paper properly.

Thick White Glue

Thick, tacky white craft glue is used to adhere heavier embellishments—it creates a much stronger bond than hot glue. Thick white glue is also the glue of choice for attaching paper-covered foam pieces in the Paper Shard Mosaic technique. (Thin-bodied glue is not as strong and dries too slowly.)

Specialty Glues

Specialty craft glues, such as jewelry and wood glues, work best for specific applications (e.g., jewelry glue for attaching buttons to a wood surface). They are white when wet and dry crystal clear.

Adhering Paper to Surfaces

Decoupage, from the French *decouper* meaning "to cut out," is the creative art of assembling, pasting, and finishing paper cutouts to decorate objects. Careful gluing will result in heirloom quality projects you'll be proud to display and give as gifts.

- **Thin Papers**

  For fine papers such as tissue and fine handmade papers, brush decoupage medium on the surface (not the paper) and position the paper piece. Immediately brush the medium over the paper to adhere and smooth out any wrinkles.

- **Medium Papers**

  For medium-weight paper pieces, use freezer paper or wax paper to protect your work surface. Lightly coat the back of the image with decoupage medium or thin-bodied glue. Position the paper on the surface and smooth with your fingers. Use a bone folder to push out wrinkles and air bubbles.

- **Larger Paper Pieces**

  Larger pieces are more likely to have bubbles and wrinkles so it's important to work fast and make sure there is an even coating of glue on the paper. Too much glue will cause excessive wrinkling that cannot be corrected.

  Use freezer paper or wax paper to protect your work surface and lightly coat the back

Using a spreading tool to apply an even coat of glue.

of the image with decoupage medium or thin-bodied glue. (TIP: Use a spreading tool to apply an even coat of glue.) Position the paper on the surface and let the glue dry before proceeding. Apply two to three coats of the decoupage medium to finish or seal with two coats of thin-bodied if you are applying a two-part polymer coating.

Tools

Have these tools on hand for all the projects.

Spreading Tool, for gluing paper to thin craft foam in the Paper Shard Mosaic technique. A handy substitute for a spreading tool is a **plastic credit card**.

Tweezers, for picking up small paper pieces. Use a sharp pointed set of tweezers for best results. An alternative tool for picking up small paper pieces is a **suction pen**, which allows you to perfectly place small paper pieces on surfaces.

Bone Folder, for removing wrinkles and creases quickly and for creating a firm bond between the paper and the surface (use the smooth sides for this).

A bone folder is especially useful when gluing large paper pieces to foam core tiles.

Air- or Water-Erase Felt Pen, for making marks on paper when cutting tiles. These pens are also useful for making lines on the base surface to keep tiles straight and square when gluing. Air-erase pen marks fade quickly; water-erase pen marks disappear when wiped with a damp cloth. Find them at fabric stores or in the sewing sections of craft stores.

Pictured left to right: tweezers, spreading tool, bone folder, air- or water-erase pen, suction pen.

Protecting Your Project

Properly protecting your finished work means that it will last, providing years of enjoyment. Make sure that if you are giving the piece as a gift that you include instructions for care.

Acrylic Varnish

On painted surfaces, two or three coats of acrylic varnish will protect and beautify the finish. Acrylic varnishes come in gloss, satin, and matte sheens, plus sepia tones, metallics, and iridescents.

Application. Roll the varnish container instead of shaking it to minimize bubbles on your finished piece. Pour the varnish in a small disposable bowl (this prevents contaminating the large container) and use a large soft brush to apply the varnish to the surface in slow, thin coats. Let each coat dry thoroughly before adding another. The more thin coats you apply, the tougher the surface will be.

Care. Simply wipe the surface with a damp cloth. For tough stains or marks, gently sand until the mark is gone with very fine grit sandpaper, remove the dust, and re-varnish the piece with at least two coats.

Dimensional Varnish

This product comes in a handy bottle with a narrow opening that allows you to squeeze the varnish on individual paper pieces. It dries clear and with a slight dimension, making the paper piece look more like a real tile. Available in clear and tinted sepia and antique hues, it is the answer to creating a shiny, dimensional mosaic piece without a polymer resin coating.

Application. After the paper pieces are decoupaged on the surface, brush on a topcoat of decoupage medium and let dry. Pour dimensional varnish on each paper piece, being careful not to let the varnish flow off the piece. (TIP: Outline each piece, then fill in the center area.) Let dry undisturbed.

Care. One disadvantage of dimensional varnish is that it is suitable for decorative purposes only. The finished surface is soft and easily damaged by water or if heavy objects are placed on top.

Decoupage Mosaics

Decoupage Mosaic is the simplest technique for creating a mosaic look. The paper pieces are glued on a prepared surface and finished with acrylic varnish or polymer coating. Applying dimensional varnish gives a more realistic mosaic appearance.

A variation of this technique, the Wood Inlay Mosaic, mimics parquetry and marquetry.

Decoupage Mosaics, Step-by-Step

1. Prepare. Prepare the surface on which you will create the mosaic. See "Techniques for Surface Preparation."

2. Cut. Cut the decorative paper into the mosaic pieces. See "Cutting Tools & Techniques."

3. Glue. Glue the paper mosaic pieces to the surface, using decoupage medium. See "Adhering Paper to Surfaces." Let dry. If finishing with a polymer resin coating, seal the surface with two coats of thin-bodied white glue.

4. Finish. Apply clear varnish or a polymer coating. See "Protecting Your project."

Decorative Mosaic Plate

For this simple project you need only one sheet of 12" x 12" memory paper.
Choose a paper design to complement your home decor.

Supplies

Surface: Wooden plate, 10" diameter

Acrylic Craft Paints: Light green-gray, metallic gold (or colors that match your paper)

Paper: Decorative memory paper, one 12" x 12" sheet

Glue: Decoupage medium

Finish: Matte acrylic varnish

Tools: Sponge, 5-1/4" circle template, Brushes for basecoating, scissors, paper trimmer, ruler

How to

1. Basecoat the plate with light green-gray paint. Let dry.
2. Using a painting sponge, rim the plate with metallic gold paint. Let dry.
3. Using a 5-1/4" circle template, cut a circle from the decorative paper. Set aside.
4. Cut small (approximately 1/2") paper pieces from the decorative paper of various shapes.
5. Decoupage the paper circle to the middle of the plate.
6. Decoupage the small paper mosaic pieces to make a border around the circle, placing them randomly. Leave small spaces between each piece to imitate grout lines.
7. Finish with two to three coats of matte varnish. ▪

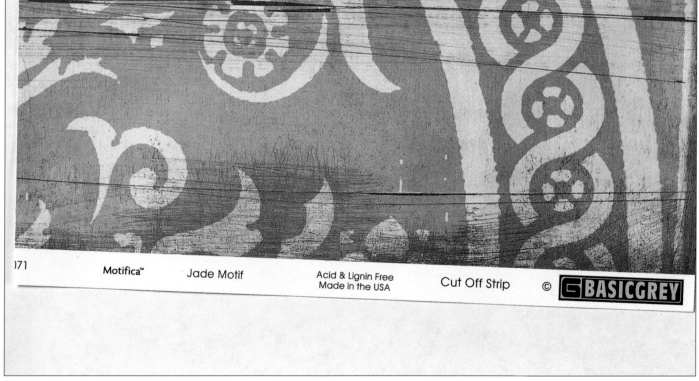

071　　Motifica™　　Jade Motif　　Acid & Lignin Free Made in the USA　　Cut Off Strip　　©　BASICGREY

Example of paper used.

Old Rose Box & Coasters

The wooden box and coasters—purchased as a set—are perfect surfaces for decoupage mosaics.
The box was finished with acrylic varnish, while the coasters have a two-part polymer coating.

Supplies

Surface: Wooden box, 5" x 5" x 2", with 4 coasters, each 4" x 4"

Acrylic Craft Paint: Antique rose

Paper: Decorative memory paper - 1 sheet each, floral and floral border

Glues: Decopauge medium, jewelry glue

Embellishments: Oval label holder, silver flower charm

Finishes: Sepia-tinted dimensional varnish, two-part polymer coating, acrylic satin varnish

Tools: Brushes, scissors, paper trimmer

How to

Paint:

Basecoat the outside of the box and all four coasters with antique rose paint. Let dry.

Decorate the Box:

1. Cut a rose image from the floral paper. Cut into mosaic pieces. Decoupage to the top of the box.
2. Cut a 3/8" border of small mosaic pieces from the same paper. Decoupage around the rose motif.
3. From the floral stripe paper, cut 1/2" mosaic pieces. Decoupage around the edge of the lid.
4. Line the inside of the box with the floral and floral striped paper, cutting the pieces to size with a paper trimmer. Decoupage in place.
5. Brush the inside and outside of the box with two coats of satin varnish. Let dry.
6. Glue the label holder to the top of the box with jewelry glue. Glue the floral charm inside the label holder.
7. Apply sepia-toned dimensional varnish inside the label holder.

Decorate the Coasters:

1. For each coaster, cut a 1-3/4" square from floral paper. Decoupage to the center of the coaster.
2. For the border of each coaster, cut four 3-3/4" x 1/4" strips of border paper. Decoupage to the edges.
3. Seal decoupaged surfaces of the coasters with white glue. Let dry.
4. Apply a two-part polymer coating. ▉

Examples of papers.

Glass Tesserae Frame

A glass tesserae effect was created on this contemporary frame with colored tissue paper. The color transfer technique (explained below) used to color the tissue paper is inexpensive and requires no paints or inks—the color comes from the colored tissue paper.

A pink picture bow was added to the frame for hanging. Samantha's cute, colorful picture completes the bright and cheerful look. Seed beads add extra sparkle and texture.

Supplies

Surface: Wooden frame, 7" x 9", with a 3-1/2" x 5-1/2" opening

Acrylic Craft Paint: White

Paper: Tissue paper in rainbow colors (See "Making Color Transfer Tissue Paper" for instructions.)

Glues: Thin white glue, thick white glue

Embellishments: Clear seed beads, pink wire-edge ribbon, 1-1/2"wide, screw eye

Finish: Pearl decoupage medium, two-part polymer coating

Tools: Brushes, scissors, decorative flower punch

How to

1. Basecoat the frame with the white paint. Let dry.
2. Make the color transfer tissue paper (see page 28), let it dry completely, and cut some of the tissue paper into strips, then into 1/2" mosaic pieces. Glue down the pieces in order using thin white glue, creating a rainbow effect. Decoupage the pieces halfway up the right side of the frame and three-quarters of the way up on the left side. Also add pieces to the sides of the frame.
3. Using a flower decorative punch, punch flowers from the colored tissue. *TIP:* Fold the tissue paper and punch through many layers—it's faster and makes a cleaner cut than cutting a single layer.
4. Adhere the tiny tissue flowers to the top part of the frame, arranging them in the rainbow color sequence.
5. Coat the tissue pieces with pearl decoupage medium. Let dry completely.
6. Seal the decoupaged surface with white glue. Let dry.
7. Apply a two-part polymer coating. When the coating has stopped flowing over the edges of the frame and is starting to set up, place a single seed bead at the middle of each tissue paper flower.
8. When the frame has fully cured, insert an eye screw at the top of the frame.
9. Loop a length of the ribbon through the eye screw to make the hanger. Make a ribbon bow and glue it in place with thick white glue, using the photo as a guide. ▦

Color transfer tissue paper, see page 30 for technique.

Wine Table Mats

In this project, the main images are surrounded with mosaic pieces. All the paper pieces were cut from the same trio of art prints. Use this idea to give new life to older mats or to decorate inexpensive table mats from a discount store.

Supplies

Surface: 3 cork-backed placemats, 8-1/2" x 11"

Acrylic Craft Paint: Deep maroon

Paper: Trio of art prints with wine-related images

Glues: Decoupage medium, thin white glue

Finish: Two-part polymer coating

Tools: Brushes, scissors, paper trimmer

How to

1. Basecoat all three mats with deep maroon paint. Let dry.
2. Cut out the main images from each print and decoupage on the mats. TIP: Work with one print and one mat at a time to avoid getting the pieces mixed up. The pieces don't need to be glued as they were in the prints, but make sure you do not run out of room as you compose the piece.
3. Cut out 3/4" mosaic "tiles" from the remaining parts of the print and decoupage to the mats. TIP: Don't worry about filling in all the spaces—part of the composition can include blank spaces to add interest. Let dry completely.
4. Seal the decoupaged surfaces with glue. Let dry.
5. Coat the mats with a two-part polymer coating. ▪▪

Glass Tesserae Frame *continued from page 28*

Making Color Transfer Tissue Paper

Choose an area to work where you will be able to leave the paper undisturbed while it is drying.

Basic Supplies

Water spritzer, filled with clean water

Freezer paper or wax paper

Colored tissue paper (You want the type labeled "bleeding tissue.")

White card paper, 8-1/2" x 11"

Procedure

1. Cut the tissue paper into pieces slightly smaller than the white card paper.
2. Protect your work area by covering with freezer paper or wax paper.
3. Place the white base paper on your work surface and spray lightly with the water. Place a piece of colored tissue on top. Spritz again lightly with water. Repeat, using different colors of tissue and spraying each piece with water, until you have piled up four to six sheets.
4. Let the pile sit and begin to dry. The dyes from the tissue sheets will mingle and mix. When the sheets are just damp, peel off the individual sheets and lay flat to continue drying. The white card paper on the bottom sheet will be beautifully colored as well—use it for card making or other paper crafting projects. TIP: Let the tissue dry completely before judging your success—the subtle patterns and colors are not entirely revealed until completely dry. ▪▪

Poker Box

Use this box to hold playing cards and game pieces. I used real playing cards and printed game pieces that I found in a scrapbooking store, but you could also color photocopy or scan and print playing pieces to decoupage on the box. I used dimensional varnish to create the raised mosaic look.

Supplies

Surface: Wooden box, 11" x 8" x 2-1/2"
Acrylic Craft Paint: Black
Paper: Playing cards, images of game pieces (e.g., bingo card, poker chips, dominos)
Glue: Decoupage medium
Embellishments: One of a pair of dice, box hinges, finishing nail
Finishes: Matte finish sealer, clear dimensional paint
Tools: Drill and drill bit, brushes

How to

1. Basecoat the box with the black paint. Let dry.
2. Cut out a poker hand and decoupage to the box top. Add the other images, using the project photo as a suggested arrangement. Leave small spaces between the paper pieces to imitate grout lines.
3. Coat the box with two to three coats of matte varnish. Let dry.
4. Coat the domino and poker chip pieces with clear dimensional paint. Let dry.
5. To make a knob for the box, drill a hole into one of a pair of dice. Attach to the box with a finishing nail.
6. Install hinges on the box. ▪

Marbled Oval Tray

This oval tray uses clear dimensional varnish to create the look of tiles. The shiny pieces on the rim contrast nicely with the textured, color washed center of the tray.

Supplies

Surface: Oval wooden tray with a wide rim, 12" x 16"

Acrylic Craft Paint: Deep teal, light green, medium green, gray (or colors to match the paper pieces)

Other Paints & Mediums: Texture paint, gel medium

Paper: 3 sheets of memory paper, piece of plain paper larger than the platter

Glue: Decoupage medium

Finishes: Clear dimensional paint, matte acrylic varnish

Tools: Scissors, brushes

How to

Make a Pattern:
Place the large piece of paper over the platter. Rub the rim to trace and create a creased image of the rim. Cut out and set aside.

Paint:
1. Apply a layer of texture paint to the inner area of the platter. Let dry.
2. Basecoat the platter and textured paint with deep teal paint. Let dry.
3. Mix the remaining paint colors with gel medium. Following the instructions in the "Techniques for Surface Preparation" section, color wash the texture-painted area.

Decoupage:
Cut the paper pattern into pieces and use it to cut mosaic pieces from decorative paper. Decoupage them in place around the rim. TIP: Cut and arrange the paper in color groups as shown.

Finish:
1. Coat the entire platter (the mosaic pieces and the color-washed texture paint) with two to three coats of matte varnish. Let dry.
2. Coat the mosaic paper pieces with clear dimensional paint. ▦

Country Star Tray

This design creates a mosaic around star-shaped patterned paper pieces. It was easy to find coordinated memory papers to create this country design. I applied a pour-on resin coating to the tray for a durable, practical surface.

Continued on page 40

Country Star Tray *continued from page 38*

Supplies

Surface: Wooden tray, 12" x 10"
Acrylic Stain: Dark brown
Paper: Blue denim, red bandanna, and red gingham decorative memory papers
Glues: Decoupage medium, thin white glue
Finish: Two-part polymer coating
Special Tools: Piece of wax, 100-grit sandpaper
Tools: Brushes, scissors, paper trimmer

How to

Distress:
See the instructions for Distressing in the Techniques for Surface Preparation section.

1. Rub tray with a piece of wax in areas where you want the paint to sand away — especially at the edges and corners.
2. Stain the tray, inside and out, with dark brown stain. Let dry.
3. Sand areas of the tray with 100-grit sandpaper. Wipe away the dust.

Decoupage:
1. Using the patterns provided, cut out six stars from blue denim paper. Decoupage in place on the bottom of the tray.
2. Cut the bandanna paper into pieces approximately 1" x 1-1/2". Decoupage around the inner edge of the tray bottom to make a border, cutting the pieces around the stars as you go.
3. Fill in the rest of the tray bottom with 1/2" mosaic pieces cut from gingham paper. Let dry.

Finish:
1. Seal the tray bottom and sides with glue. Let dry.
2. Coat with the tray bottom and sides with the two-part polymer coating. ▟

Paper examples.

Country Star Tray Patterns

Little Blue Box

*I used a paper punch to create the mosaic "tiles." The medallions are cut from
a color-blended origami paper called* Bokashi, *which means shading.*

Supplies

Surface: Wooden box, 4-1/2" square,
   2-1/2" tall
Acrylic Craft Paint: Country blue,
   gold
Paper: Origami paper, cut into 2"
   squares
Glue: Thin white glue
Embellishment: Wooden knob
Finishes: Sepia-tone decoupage
   medium, two-part polymer
   coating, satin varnish
Tools: Corner fleur de lis decorative punch, brushes

How to

1. Basecoat the outside of the box and lid and the wooden knob with
   country blue paint. Let dry.
2. Basecoat the inside of the box and lid with gold paint. Let dry.
3. Fold and punch the origami squares with the Fleur de lis corner punch
   to create four medallions.
4. Decoupage the medallions to the box top with sepia-toned decoupage finish. Let dry.
5. Seal the lid of the box with glue. Let dry.
6. Apply the two-part polymer coating. When the coating starts to set
   up, place the knob into the still-sticky coating at the center of the
   mosaic design. (When the coating is cured, the knob will be securely
   fastened.)
7. Brush the box base with two to three coats of satin varnish. Let dry
   between coats. ❖

Photo Mosaic Tray

Photographs can be used to create lovely personalized gifts that are sure to become family treasures. The photographs on this tray are cut with a paper trimmer and decoupaged in place.

Supplies

Surface: Wooden tray, 11" x 15"

Acrylic Craft Paint: Soft tan, golden brown (or colors to match your photographs)

Paper: Photocopies or printouts of photographs, shell motifs cut from decoupage paper

Glues: Decoupage medium, thin white glue

Finishes: Two-part polymer coating, matte varnish

Tools: Brushes, paper trimmer, scissors

How to

1. Basecoat the inner area of the tray with golden brown paint.
2. Basecoat the outside of the tray with soft tan paint.
3. Using a paper trimmer, cut out the focal point of each photo. Decoupage in place, using the photo as a guide.
4. Cut additional squares from photographs and placed around the focal point pieces. Leave some blank spaces for the shell motifs.
5. Cut out the shell motifs and decoupage to the tray. Let dry.
6. Seal the inside bottom and rim of the tray with glue. Let dry.
7. Apply a two-part polymer coating to the decoupaged area of the tray. Let dry and cure.
8. Varnish the (uncoated) outside of the tray with matte varnish. ⊞

Renaissance Box

This elegant piece uses decoupage paper printed with images of the paintings in Michelangelo's Sistine Chapel. The paper was cut into shaped pieces and glued in order. Some of the clock face isn't covered with paper to improve the visibility of the clock hands.

Supplies

Surface: Wooden clock, 9" x 8" with gold hands

Acrylic Craft Paint Dark sage green, light sage green, gray-green, metallic gold

Other Paints & Mediums: Texture paint, gel medium

Paper: Decoupage paper

Glues: Decoupage medium, thin white glue

Finishes: Two-part polymer coating, satin varnish

Tools: Brushes, sponge, scissors

How to

Paint:

1. Remove the center panel of the clock.
2. Brush texture paint over the sides and inner frame. Let dry.
3. Basecoat the entire clock (base and inside panel) with dark sage green paint.
4. Mix the gel medium with the other two green paints. Color wash the texture paint and the center panel, following the instructions in the Techniques for Surface Preparation section. Let dry.
5. Using a painting sponge with gold paint, add gold highlights to the edges and textured part of the clock base.
6. Finish the clock base with two to three coats of satin varnish.

Decoupage:

Cut shaped mosaic pieces from the paper and decoupage in the order of the original print on the center panel. See the project photo for placement.

Finish:

1. Seal the decoupaged panel with glue.
2. Coat the panel with two-part polymer coating.
3. While the polymer coating is still sticky, insert the decoupaged clock panel into the clock base. (This will permanently attach it to the clock.) Let cure completely.
4. Add the clock hands and clock mechanism to the clock base. ▪

Paper examples.

Faux Marquetry Grape Plate

Wood Inlay Mosaic is a variation of the Decoupage Mosaic technique. Papers printed with wood patterns and colors or very thin wood veneers are used to make the mosaic pieces. Marquetry is a style of woodworking that uses wood or wood veneer pieces to form pictorial images. It was a popular technique for fine furniture decoration in the 17th century.

This grape design on a wooden plate is simple, but the result is dramatic. The plate was not painted. A computer was used to generate the pattern for the lettering.

Supplies

Surface: Wooden plate, 14" diameter

Acrylic Craft Paint: Metallic gold

Wood Veneer: Dark cherry, medium oak, light pine

Paper: Tracing paper

Glues: Decoupage medium, thin white glue

Finish: Two-part polymer coating

Tools: Computer and printer, sponge, pencil, scissors

How to

1. Highlight the edges of the plate with metallic gold paint, using a painting sponge.
2. Trace the grape pattern. (You'll find it on the following pages.)
3. Generate a pattern for the lettering by typing the words into a computer and printing them out in 80 point Copperplate Gothic Bold.
4. Use the patterns to cut the pieces from the three colors of wood veneer:
   Grapes and lettering - Dark cherry
   Leaves - Medium oak
   Highlights on the grapes and stem - Light pine
5. Use decoupage medium to adhere the pieces to the plate. Let dry.
6. Seal the entire plate with white glue.
7. Apply a two-part polymer coating. ▄▄

Patterns are on pages 52 & 53.

Faux Marquetry Grape Plate

continued from page 48

MEHEZ LA BONNE VIE!

LIVE THE GOOD LIFE!

Faux Parquetry Frame

Parquetry is a wood inlay technique that uses wood veneers to create geometric designs. This framed mirror may look complicated, but it is simple to make. I used a decorative punch and wood-printed decorative paper to create the parquetry design. Start with a purchased dark wood frame or stain an unfinished frame the wood tone of your choice.

Supplies

Surface: Wood frame, 10" x 10", with 3-1/2" square opening

Stain: optional, Dark mahogany or walnut

Paper: Decorative paper printed with wood designs in medium and light tones

Glues: Decoupage medium, thin white glue

Embellishment: Mirror, 3-1/2" square

Tools: Mosaic decorative punch, fleur de lis decorative punch, brushes, paper trimmer, scissors

How to

1. *Option:* Stain the frame. Let dry.
2. Cut the medium-tone wood paper into a strip 1-1/2" x 10". Punch eight motifs along the strip, using the mosaic punch. Using scissors, cut each motif from the paper strip, leaving a small (1/8") border.
3. Cut the light-tone wood paper into a strip 1-1/4" x 10". Cut into eight 1-1/4"squares.
4. Decoupage the paper pieces on the frame, alternating the light squares and the punched medium-tone motifs.
5. Cut small strips (1/4" x 1-1/2") of both papers. Decoupage around the larger pieces to make a narrow border.
6. Punch four fleur de lis shapes from the medium-tone paper. Decoupage to the corners.
7. Seal the entire surface of the frame with white glue. Let dry.
8. Apply a two-part polymer coating.
9. When cured, insert and glue the mirror in the frame opening. ❖

Energy Swirl Box

This box design imitates the look of glass tesserae. The Color Transfer Tissue Paper technique was used to color the paper shards that are arranged on a dark purple surface.

Supplies

Surface: Wooden box, 5-3/4" square, 3-3/4" tall

Acrylic Craft Paint: Purple, white, pink, and acrylic gel medium

Paper & Foam: White thin craft foam, color transfer tissue paper (See the instructions for Making Color Transfer Tissue Paper with the Glass Tesserae Frame project.)

Glues: Thin white glue, thick white glue

Embellishments: Brass label holder, dragonfly stickers, sticker letters

Finish: Pearl decoupage medium, 3 oz. two-part polymer coating

Tools: Brushes, scissors

How to

1. Basecoat the box top and bottom with purple paint. Let dry.
2. Mix the three paint colors with gel medium and color wash the sides of the box bottom. Let dry.
3. Decoupage the box bottom with hearts cut from the color transfer tissue paper.
4. Paint swirls with the purple gel medium mix to decorate the bottom of the box.
5. Glue the colored tissue paper on the white foam.
6. Brush with pearl decoupage medium. Let dry. Apply a second coat and let dry.
7. Cut the paper into irregular shards approximately 1/2" in size.
8. Paint a swirl design on the box top with pearl decoupage medium. Glue the paper shards on the box top in the swirl pattern. Let dry.
9. Seal the mosaic design with a coat of white glue. Let dry.
10. Apply a two-part polymer coating to the top. Let dry and cure.
11. Decorate the box bottom with the brass label holder and the dragonflies. Use jewelry glue to adhere them. ▟

Red Floral Frame

Matching decorative papers with floral designs make these paper mosaic shards look like broken china pieces. The addition of the found objects (the key and buttons) is reminiscent Victorian memory ware mosaics. The resulting frame has an antique appearance, perfect for a favorite vintage photograph.

Supplies

Surface: Wooden frame, 10" square, with a 3" square opening

Acrylic Craft Paints: Dark sage green, dark maroon

Papers & Foam: Solid dark red, two coordinating red floral patterns, white thin craft foam

Glues: Jewelry glue, thin white glue, thick white glue

Embellishments: Red buttons, key, keyhole

Finish: 4 oz. two-part polymer coating

Tools: Brushes, water-erase pen, scissors

How to

Paint & Prepare:

1. Basecoat the frame with dark sage green paint. Let dry.
2. Position the key and keyhole on the frame and trace around the shapes with a water-erase felt marker. Paint inside these tracings with dark maroon paint. Let dry.
3. Glue the key and keyhole in place with jewelry glue.

Create the Mosaic:

1. Glue the decorative papers to the craft foam. Apply a second coat of glue to seal. Let dry.
2. Cut the paper shards in irregular shapes 1/2" to 3/4" in size.
3. Glue the paper shards on the frame, using the solid red shards to frame the opening. Glue buttons among the shards. Continue gluing paper shards, leaving larger empty spaces as you approach the frame edge.

Finish:

1. Seal the entire frame with white glue. Let dry.
2. Apply a two-part polymer coating. ▪

Paper examples.

Shard Mosaic Frame

This paper shard frame has a contemporary look. A small metal plaque with a charming saying accents the composition. You can find metal embellishments at scrapbooking and crafts stores.

Supplies

Surface: Wooden frame, 10"square, with a 3" square opening

Acrylic Craft Paint: White

Paper & Foam: Four coordinated decorative green papers, white thin craft foam

Glues: Thin white glue, thick white glue, jewelry glue

Embellishment: Metal plaque with saying, 1-1/2" x 2-1/2"

Finish:4 oz. two-part polymer coating

Tools: Brushes, scissors

How to

Prepare:

1. Basecoat the frame with the white paint. Let dry.
2. Glue the metal plaque in place with jewelry glue.

Create the Mosaic:

1. Glue the decorative papers to the foam. Apply a second seal coat of glue. Let dry.
2. Cut out the mosaic paper shards in irregular shapes about 3/4" square.
3. Glue the paper shards over the entire front of the frame. Let dry.

Finish:

1. Seal the entire frame with white glue. Let dry.
2. Apply a two-part polymer coating. ■

Paper examples.

What one loves
in childhood
stays in your
heart
forever

~Mary Jo Putney

Sea Shell Frame

This mosaic mirror frame, in the pique assiette *tradition, uses real seashells and a dried starfish along with the paper shards. It would make a charming addition to a beach cottage or sea-themed bathroom.*

Supplies

Surface: Wooden frame, 10" square, with a 3-1/2" opening

Acrylic Craft Paint & Medium: Blue acrylic paint and gel medium, mixed in equal amounts to make a transparent blue stain

Paper & Foam: Natural colored handmade paper, fish decoupage paper, white thin craft foam

Glues: Thin white glue, thick white glue

Embellishments: Shells, dried starfish, mirror to fit frame opening

Finish: 4 oz. two-part polymer coating

Tools: Brushes, scissors

How to

1. Stain the frame with the blue stain.
2. Glue the decorative papers to the foam. Apply a second coat of glue to seal. Let dry.
3. Cut irregularly shaped mosaic shards, about 3/4" in size.
4. Glue the paper shards, shells, and starfish in place on the frame.
5. Seal the entire frame with white glue. Let dry.
6. Apply a two-part polymer coating. ❖

Paper examples.

Scalloped Edge Tray

This tray was made to match a blue floral tea set—I chose the papers to match the china. The paper shards form a mosaic rim with a plain painted center that can hold all the makings for a quiet cup of tea.

Continued on page 70.

Scalloped Edge Tray continued from page 68

Supplies

Surface: Wooden tray with scalloped edge

Acrylic Craft Paint: Light ivory

Paper & Foam: Four coordinated blue patterned papers, white thin craft foam

Glues: Thin white glue, thick white glue

Finish: 6 oz. two-part polymer coating

Tools: Brushes, scissors, water-erase pen

How to

1. Basecoat the platter with light ivory paint. Let dry.
2. Glue the decorative papers to the foam. Apply a second coat of glue to seal. Let dry.
3. Cut irregularly shaped mosaic shards, about 3/4" in size.
4. Using the project photo as a guide, draw the spaces for the groups of shards with a water-erase felt marker on the rim of the platter.
5. Glue the paper shards in color groups around the rim of the platter.
6. Seal the entire frame with white glue. Let dry.
7. Apply a two-part polymer coating. ▉

Paper examples.

Fruit Tray

Pictured on pages 72 & 73.

This tray uses large and small paper shard mosaic pieces in one design. The larger pieces are glued in sequence to retain the composition of the fruit motifs. Smaller paper shards, glued randomly, fill the remaining spaces.

With a resin coating, this tray is a practical and welcome addition to your kitchen (or someone else's).

Supplies

Surface: Wooden tray, 9" x 18"
Acrylic Craft Paints: White, celery green, dark sage
Paper & Foam: Fruit decoupage paper, white thin craft foam
Glues: Thin white glue, thick white glue
Finish: 6 oz. two-part polymer coating
Tools: Brushes, scissors

Continued on page 72.

Paper examples.

Fruit Tray *continued from page 71*

How to

Paint:
1. Basecoat the tray edges with white paint.
2. Basecoat the tray bottom with celery green.
3. Basecoat the handles with dark sage.

Create the Mosaic:
1. Glue the decoupage paper to the foam. Apply a second coat of glue to seal. Let dry.
2. Cut the parts of the paper with fruit motifs into large irregular shards (2" to 2-1/2").
3. Cut smaller (1/2") paper shards from the same paper.
4. Using the photo as a guide, glue the larger paper shards in place, keeping the fruit motifs intact.
5. Fill the remaining spaces with smaller paper shard pieces. Let dry.

Finish:
1. Seal the entire platter with white glue. Let dry.
2. Apply a two-part polymer coating. ▟

Ancient
Asian Ladies Canvas

*On this piece, the tiles overhang the edges of the canvas board used for the base.
I used varnish crackle on the paper pieces so the appearance is
like that of cracked glaze on ancient tiles.*

Supplies

Surface: Canvas board, 12" square

Paper: Asian ladies decoupage paper

Glue: Thin white glue

Foam Core Board: 3/16"

Acrylic Craft Paint: Black, brown stain

Finishes: Varnish crackle medium, 15 oz. two-part polymer coating

Tools: Brushes, art knife, cutting mat, ruler

How to

1. Trim the paper into tiles. Cut two additional ladies to embellish two tiles with Asian characters.
2. Using the paper pieces as patterns, cut the foam core board into pieces exactly the same size as the paper tile pieces.
3. Glue the foam core tiles in place on the canvas board. Let dry.
4. Paint the foam core tiles and canvas board with black paint. Let dry.
5. Glue the paper pieces to the corresponding foam core tiles.
6. Glue the two figure cutouts to two tiles, using the photo as a guide.
7. Following the instructions in the Techniques for Surface Preparation section, apply crackle varnish to the tiles.
8. Apply antiquing where you want the crackles to appear. Let dry.
9. Seal the entire piece (tiles and canvas board) with two coats of thin-bodied white glue.
10. Apply a two-art resin coating. ⊞

Provence Landscape Napkin Box

This is a very easy project—it has just four tiles. It's a good idea to start with a project like this one—you'll gain confidence to tackle larger projects, which you'll find aren't all that difficult either.

Coincidentally, I found napkins with the same image as my print to place inside my napkin box!

Supplies

Surface: Wooden napkin box, 7" square, 2" tall
Paper: Landscape art print
Glue: Thin white glue
Foam core: 3/16"
Acrylic Craft Paint: Dark terra cotta
Finishes: 4 oz. two-part polymer coating, matte vanish
Tools: Brushes, art knife, cutting mat, ruler

How to

1. Cut the print into four 3-1/4" square pieces.
2. Using the paper pieces as patterns, cut the foam core board exactly the same size as the paper pieces.
3. Glue the foam core tiles in place on the top of the box. Let dry.
4. Basecoat the tiles and box surface with dark terra cotta paint. Let dry.
5. Glue the paper pieces to their matching-size tiles. Let dry.
6. Seal the tiles and the top of the box with white glue. Let dry.
7. Apply a two-part polymer coating to the top of the box. Let cure.
8. Seal the rest of the box with matte varnish. ▉

— Tonight —
- baby field greens
- Calamari fritti
- roast chicken w/
  fig balsamic
  reduction
- assorted cheeses
- lemon sorbet
- grappa

Wine Club
Tasting Sat.

POSTCARD

Sarah Martin
264 Oak St.
Atlanta
Ga

A-B-C
Child's Table

Tile art transformed a simple wooden table into a delightful accent for a child's room. A matching wooden chair was painted with the same colors and decoupaged with coordinated decorative paper. You can find the letter cutouts in a variety of colors in the scrapbooking departments of crafts stores.

Continued on page 86

ABC Child's Table

continued from page 84

Supplies

Surface: Wooden table, 15-1/2" square, 16" high

Paper: Country landscape memory paper, 12" x 12", plus more for the chair; coordinating yellow and butterfly motif papers; alphabet letters

Glues: Thin white glue, decoupage medium

Foam Core Board: 3/16" white

Acrylic Craft Paints: Soft yellow, light lilac, medium lilac

Finishes: 10 oz. two-part polymer coating, gloss varnish

Tools: Brushes, art knife, cutting mat, ruler, scissors

Table:

1. Cut four 5-1/2" square tiles from the sheet of country landscape paper.
2. Cut four strips, each 1-1/2" x 12", from yellow decorative paper for the border.
3. Cut four 1-1/2" square tiles from butterfly motif paper for the corners of the border.
4. Using the paper pieces as patterns, cut the foam core board into pieces exactly the same sizes as the paper pieces.
5. Glue the foam core tiles in place on the table top. Let dry.
6. Basecoat the table top with medium lilac paint.
7. Paint the table legs with light lilac.
8. Paint the table apron with soft yellow.
9. Glue the paper pieces to their matching-size tiles.
10. Decoupage the letters to the border tiles.
11. Cut out four butterflies from the butterfly motif paper. Decoupage on the center tiles, using the photo as a guide for placement.
12. Seal the tiles and the table top with white glue. Let dry.
13. Apply a two-part polymer coating to the table top.
14. Finish the table apron and legs with two coats gloss varnish.

Chair:

1. Paint the chair seat with medium lilac.
2. Paint the vertical pieces with soft yellow.
3. Paint the horizontal pieces with light lilac. Let dry.
4. Cut out images from the landscape paper and a few butterflies from the butterfly paper.
5. Use decoupage medium to adhere the cutouts to the chair back, using the photo as a guide for placement. Let dry.
6. Seal the chair with two or more coats gloss varnish. ▉

Paper examples

Spice Cabinet

This wooden cabinet makes a great kitchen accent and holds jars and packages of herbs and spices. A single sheet of paper was used to create the tiles on the recessed panel of the door. The surface was painted, then stained for an antique look.

Supplies

Surface: Wooden spice cabinet, 14" x 20" x 4"

Paper: 1 sheet printed memory paper

Glue: Thin white glue

Foam Core Board: 3/16" white

Acrylic Craft Paints: Ochre, dark green, dark burgundy, dark brown stain

Embellishment: Brass knob

Finishes: 6 oz. two-part polymer coating, satin varnish

Tools: Brushes, art knife, cutting mat, ruler

How to

1. Cut the memory paper into six pieces to fit inside the recessed panel of the door. (Mine are 5" x 4".)
2. Using the paper pieces as patterns, cut the foam core board into pieces exactly the same sizes as the paper pieces.
3. Glue the foam core tiles to the recessed panel of the cabinet door. Let dry.
4. Basecoat the tiles and recessed door panel with dark burgundy paint.
5. Basecoat the front and sides of the cabinet with ochre paint.
6. Paint the trim with dark green. Let dry.
7. Apply brown stain to the ochre and green painted areas for an antique look. Let dry.
8. Glue the paper pieces to their matching-size tiles. Let dry.
9. Seal the tiles and door panel with thin white glue. Let dry.
10. Apply a two-part polymer coating to the tiles and the recessed panel of the door.
11. Seal the remainder of the cabinet with two coats satin varnish. ■

Tuscan Landscape Canvas

This dramatic wall piece uses a single art print for the tiles. The textured surface that frames the tiles was finished with a matte spray for contrast.

Supplies

Surface: Archival canvas board, 18" x 24"

Paper: Tuscan villa art print

Foam Core Board: 1/2" white

Acrylic Craft Paints: Texture paint, dark terra cotta, ochre, terra cotta, Gel medium

Embellishment: Metal label holder, piece of trimmed paper, wooden frame

Finishes: 10 oz. two-part polymer coating, matte sealer spray

Tools: Calligraphy marker, brushes, art knife, cutting mat, ruler

How to

1. Cut the print into four 6" square pieces.
2. Using the paper pieces as patterns, cut the 1/2" foam core board into pieces exactly the same sizes as the paper pieces.
3. Glue the foam core in place on the canvas board, 3-1/2" from the top and centered.
4. Brush texture paint on the canvas board around the tiles. Let dry.
5. Basecoat the foam core tiles and textured area with dark terra cotta paint.
6. Following the instructions in the Techniques for Surface Preparation section, color wash the textured area with the remaining paint colors.
7. Trim a piece of paper left over from the print to fit the label holder. With a calligraphy marker, write the name of the city or the artist on the paper.
8. Glue the label holder on the canvas board with jewelry glue.
9. Place the paper label in the label holder.
10. Glue the paper pieces to their matching-size foam core tiles. Let dry.
11. Seal the entire surface with white glue. Let dry.
12. Apply a two-part polymer coating. When the bubbles have been removed from the coating and it has stopped flowing over the edges, position the frame on the canvas board.
13. When the coating has completely cured, place wax paper over the tiles and spray the textured area with matte sealer. ⊞

Domestico

Paris Vacation Photo Tray

Cherished photos from a Paris vacation and decorative memory papers decorate this stylish tray. Since the tray was purchased finished, no basecoating was required. Using black foam core board eliminated having to paint the tiles. This tray was created by Jean Laturnus. It was her first tile art project.

Supplies

Surface: Wooden tray, 11-1/2" x 18", stained and varnished

Paper: Photocopies or printouts of photographs, decorative papers

Glue: Thin white glue

Foam Core Board: 3/16" black

Embellishments: Rub-on letters, stamps, and rub-on motifs

Finish: 6 oz. two-part polymer coating

Tools: Brushes, art knife, cutting mat, ruler

How to

1. Trim the photographs and memory paper into shapes to fit the bottom of the tray.
2. Decorate these paper pieces with rub-on letters or motifs to add interest.
3. Using the paper pieces as patterns, cut foam core board pieces exactly the same sizes as the paper pieces.
4. Glue the foam core pieces in place on the bottom of the tray. Let dry.
5. Glue the paper pieces to their matching-shape foam core tiles.
6. Seal the tiles and the bottom of the tray with white glue. Let dry.
7. Apply the two-part polymer coating. Brush the excess up the sides of the tray but not over the tray edge. ◨

Accent Table

A favorite print gives new life to an occasional table; the space around the print was filled with tiles covered with handmade papers. With this method, you can make any print fit your desired base surface.

The table now matches the new decor of the room where it's proudly displayed by its creator, Sharon Ritchie.

Supplies

Surface: Table with top measuring 12-1/2" x 18"

Papers: Art print from wall calendar, handmade natural papers in brown and ochre hues

Glue: Thin white glue

Foam Core Board: 3/16" white

Acrylic Craft Paint: Dark brown

Finish: 10 oz. two-part polymer coating

Tools: Brushes, art knife, cutting mat, ruler

How to

1. Cut the print into four 5" square tiles.
2. Cut the handmade papers in pieces to create tiles that fill in the remaining space on the table top.
3. Using the paper pieces as the patterns, cut the foam core board in pieces exactly the same sizes as the paper tile pieces.
4. Glue the foam core tiles in place on the table top. Let dry.
5. Basecoat the tiles and table top with dark brown paint. Let dry.
6. Glue on the paper pieces to their matching-size tiles.
7. Seal the tiles and table top with white glue. Let dry.
8. Apply a two-part polymer coating to the entire table top. ▓

Shattered Canvas

The Shattered Tile Art technique uses both 1/2" and 3/16" thick foam core boards to create tiles of different heights. For best results, choose a print with an abstract image.

This project was created by Sharon Ritchie. It is her first tile art project.

Supplies

Surface: Archival canvas board, 16" x 20"; wooden frame to fit finished piece
Paper: Abstract art print
Glue: Thin white glue
Foam Core Board: 1/2" and 3/16"
Acrylic Craft Paint: Black
Finish: 12 oz. two-part polymer coating
Tools: Brushes, art knife, cutting mat, ruler

How to

1. Cut the print into seven or eight irregular shapes. Use the images on the print as a guide when deciding where to cut. In your calculation for size, include a 1/2" border on all sides to allow for the lip of the frame.
2. Using the paper pieces as patterns, cut pieces of foam core board exactly the same sizes as the paper pieces. Cut at least three pieces from 1/2" foam core board.
3. Glue the foam core tiles in place on the canvas board, keeping all tiles at least 1/2" from the edges. Let dry.
4. Basecoat the tiles and canvas board with black paint. Let dry.
5. Glue the paper pieces to their matching-size tiles.
6. Seal the tiles and canvas board with white glue. Let dry.
7. Coat the entire piece with two-part polymer coating. When the coating has been de-gassed and has stopped flowing over the edge, place the frame in place over the canvas board. ▪

Tropical Ships Canvas

For tile art, choose art prints that accent and add drama to your rooms. The print for this wall piece was cut to create an interesting composition that includes border tiles.

This project is courtesy of Hilary Stephens of Environmental Technology, Inc.

Supplies

Surface: Archival canvas board, 16" x 20": black wooden frame to fit piece
Paper: Art print
Glue: Thin white glue
Foam Core Board: 3/16"
Acrylic Craft Paint: Black
Finish: 12 oz. two-part polymer coating
Tools: Brushes, art knife, cutting mat, ruler

How to

1. Using the project photo as a guide, cut the print into pieces. In your calculation for size, include a 1/2" border on all sides to allow for the lip of the frame.
2. Using the paper pieces as patterns, cut pieces of foam core board exactly the same sizes as the paper pieces.
3. Glue the foam core tiles in place on the canvas board, keeping the tiles at least 1/2" from the edges. Let dry.
4. Basecoat the tiles and canvas board with the black paint. Let dry.
5. Glue the paper pieces to their matching-size tiles.
6. Seal the tiles and canvas board with white glue. Let dry.
7. Coat the entire piece with two-part polymer coating. When the coating has been de-gassed and has stopped flowing over the edge, place the frame over the canvas board. ⚏

Bar Art

The black lines on the print provided guidance for creative cutting. Look for prints with large shapes to create this type of piece. A heat cutter is highly recommended for cutting the curved tile pieces.

This project is courtesy of Hilary Stephens of Environmental Technology, Inc.

Supplies

Surface: 2 plywood panels, each 9" x 15"

Paper: Art print with large shapes

Glue: Thin white glue

Foam Core Board: Tiles: 3/16" white

Acrylic Craft Paint: Black

Finish: 6 oz. two-part polymer coating per panel

Tools: Heat cutter (heated art knife), brushes, art knife, cutting mat, ruler

How to

1. Cut the print into shaped tiles, using the images as guides.
2. Using the paper pieces as patterns, cut pieces of foam core board exactly the same sizes as the paper pieces. For best results, use a heat cutter.
3. Glue the foam core tiles in place on the plywood panels. Let dry.
4. Basecoat the tiles and boards with black paint. Let dry.
5. Glue the paper pieces on their matching-shape tiles.
6. Seal the tiles and plywood panels with white glue. Let dry.
7. Coat both pieces with two-part polymer coating. ▉

Fashion Frame

This project uses images from fashion-theme greeting cards and metal die-cut words as accents. The frame, which was purchased with a stain-and-varnish finish, did not require painting or staining.

Olivia Ritchie, age 11, created this project. She had a little help with cutting the foam core board and pouring the two-part polymer coating. She applied the glue and decided how to place the pieces herself.

Supplies

Surface: Stained and varnished wood frame, 10" x 10"
Paper: Greeting cards
Glue: Thin white glue
Foam Core Board: 3/16" black
Embellishments: Metal die-cut words, metal key charm, mirror cut to fit frame opening
Finish: 4 oz. two-part polymer coating
Tools: Art knife, cutting mat, ruler

How to

1. Trim the cards into shapes for the tiles.
2. Using the paper pieces as patterns, cut pieces of foam core board exactly the same sizes as the paper pieces.
3. Glue the foam core tiles in place on the frame.
4. With jewelry glue, attach the metal words and charm to the frame. Let dry.
5. Glue the paper pieces on their matching-shape tiles.
6. Seal the tiles and frame with white glue. Let dry.
7. Coat with two-part polymer coating.
8. When the coating is fully cured, install the mirror and secure with jewelry glue. ▪

Memory Tile Art

The Memory Tile Art technique uses the framed boards specially designed to hold scrapbook pages for display on the wall, which come in 8-1/2" x 11" and 12" x 12" sizes. The backboards are covered with decorative paper, and you design the Tile Art as you would a scrapbook page, with photographs mounted on the tiles.

Black foam core board is used for the tiles so no basecoat is required. You can use actual photographs, computer printouts, or color photocopies. If you use photographs printed on an inkjet printer, seal the ink with two coats of clear spray varnish to avoid smearing.

Basketball Memory Tile Art

Photographs of the team and the individual player are displayed on decorative paper that is printed to look like a basketball court. Letter stickers add names and motivational sayings; metal embellishments are added to the frame and backboard. The space at upper right could display a medal, another player's photo, or a photo of the coach or a trophy.

Supplies

Surface: Memory frame, 11" x 13" (inside area 8-1/2" x 11")

Paper: Photographs, basketball court printed paper

Glues: Thin white glue, decoupage medium

Foam Core Board: 3/16" black

Acrylic Craft Paint: Dark terra cotta

Embellishments: Sayings stickers, gold alphabet stickers, label holder, metal alphabet stencils

Finish: 4 oz. two-part polymer coating

Tools: Brushes, art knife, cutting mat, ruler

How to

1. Trim the memory paper to fit the frame. Crop the photographs.
2. Using the cropped photographs as patterns, cut pieces of foam core board exactly the same sizes as the photos.
3. Basecoat frame with dark terra cotta paint. Let dry.
4. Decoupage the decorative paper to the inside of the frame. Let dry.
5. Glue the foam core tiles in place on the paper-covered base. Let dry.
6. Glue the photographs to their matching tiles.
7. Add letter stickers, sayings, or embellishments to the frame and/or the paper-covered area.
8. Seal the tiles, the paper-covered area, and the inside rim of the frame with white glue. Let dry.
9. Coat the tiles and the top section with two-part polymer coating. Brush the excess up the sides but not over the frame. ▪

JON

TEAM

WORK

ALL STARS

Individual commitment to a group effort—
that is what makes a **TEAM WORK.**
Vince Lombardi

PENINSULA
BASKETBALL
2001 & 02
U 13 BOYS
PEDIGREE

2001-02

Vintage Memory Tile Art

Here, vintage photographs are the focal point of this display. Scrapbooking magazines and books are a great source of page ideas for arranging photos.

Use color photocopies of photographs to preserve your originals.

Supplies

Surface: Memory frame, 11" x 13" (inside area 8-1/2" x 11")

Paper: Old photographs, vintage letters memory paper

Glues: Thin white glue, decoupage medium

Foam Core Board: 3/16" black

Acrylic Stain: Dark brown

Embellishments: Old key on black satin cord, vintage key, buttons, stickers, label holder, upholstery tack

Finish: 4 oz. two-part polymer coating

Tools: Calligraphy marker, brushes, art knife, cutting mat, ruler

How to

1. Trim the memory paper to fit the frame. Crop the photographs.
2. Using the cropped photographs as patterns, cut pieces of foam core board exactly the same sizes as the photos.
3. Stain the frame with dark brown stain. Let dry.
4. Decoupage the memory paper to the inside of the frame. Let dry.
5. Glue the foam core tiles on top of the paper-covered base. Let dry.
6. Glue the photographs to their matching tiles.
7. Add stickers, the key, and the buttons to finish the collage.
8. Seal the tiles, the paper-covered area, and the inside rim of the frame with white glue. Let dry.
9. Coat the tiles and the top section with two-part polymer coating. Brush the excess up the sides but not over the frame. Let cure.
10. Attach the label holder. Cut a piece of paper to fit the label holder, write a caption, and insert in the holder.
11. Use an upholstery tack to attach the key on the cord to one side of the frame. ▟

Photo Display Tile Art

This technique uses foam core board to display cherished photographs or a favorite print. These unique pieces are embellished with stickers, rub-on transfers, or coordinating motifs cut from decorative papers.

Photo Display Tile Art, Step-by-Step

1. **Choose the papers and embellishments.** Select a photo or print and choose coordinating memory paper. Select stickers or other embellishments.

2. **Cut the tiles.** Cut a piece of foam core board for the base. Cut smaller tiles cut from 1/2" or 3/16" foam core.

3. **Paint.** Paint the tiles, including all the edges. If the foam core tile will be covered with paper, paint only the edges. TIP: If the foam core tiles warp, paint the back and let dry. They should lay flat again.

4. **Glue:** Work from the bottom up—first glue the paper background to the base tile, then glue the next tile on top. Continue gluing papers and tiles in order. Line up the edges of the tiles or stack them at an angle for interest.

5. **Decorate.** Glue or apply embellishments and/or stickers.

6. **Seal.** Seal the entire piece with two coats of thin-bodied white glue, making sure to cover the area where the paper meets the edge of the foam core tiles. Let dry completely.

7. **Apply the coating.** Pour on the two-part polymer coating. Let cure.

Painting the tile.

Gluing the tiles together.

Here Comes Trouble!

Find a photo of your favorite little one and create a wonderful gift for parents or grandparents. The angled placement adds movement and fun.

Supplies

Paper: Denim background photo of your choice, 5" x 7"

Glue: Thin white glue

Foam Core Board: 1/2", 3/16"

Acrylic Craft Paint: Dark terra cotta

Embellishments: "Here Comes Trouble" rub-on

Finish: 5 oz. two-part polymer coating

Tools: Brushes, art knife, cutting mat, ruler

How to

Base Tile:
1. Cut a 12" square from 1/2" foam core board.
2. Paint the edges with dark terra cotta acrylic paint. Let dry.
3. Cover with denim decorative paper.
4. Embellish with a "Here Comes Trouble" rub-on. Use the photo as a guide for placement.

Frame Tile:
1. Cut a 6" x 8-1/2" tile from 3/16" foam core board.
2. Basecoat with dark terra cotta acrylic paint. Let dry.
3. Glue on the base tile at an angle, using the photo as a guide for placement.

Photo Tile:
1. Cut a 5" x 7" tile from 3/16" foam core board.
2. Paint the edges with dark terra cotta acrylic paint. Let dry.
3. Glue on the frame tile at an angle.
4. Adhere the photo to the tile.

Finish:
1. Seal the entire piece with two coats of thin-bodied glue. Let dry.
2. Pour on the two-part polymer coating. ▪▪

Wild Joy

A photo of a charming child is a perfect companion for the inspiring saying, bright daisies, and clean, clear colors!

Supplies

Paper: Photo of your choice, 4" x 5-1/2"; yellow paper with daisies
Glue: Thin white glue
Foam Core Board: 1/2", 3/16"
Acrylic Craft Paints: Soft yellow, light lilac
Embellishments: Sticker with saying on a clear backing, daisy sticker, 1/2" wide border stickers
Finish: 5 oz. two-part polymer coating
Tools: Brushes, art knife, cutting mat, ruler

How to

Base Tile:
1. Cut a 12" square from 1/2" foam core board.
2. Paint the edges with soft yellow acrylic paint. Let dry.
3. Cover with daisy paper.

Frame Tile:
1. Cut a 7-1/2" square tile from 1/2" foam core board.
2. Paint the edges and surface with light lilac acrylic paint. Let dry.
3. Glue on the base tile, using the photo as a guide for placement.
4. Embellish with daisy stickers.

Photo Tile:
1. Cut the photo off the front of the card.
2. Cut a tile 4" x 5-1/2" from 1/2" foam core board.
3. Paint the edges with soft yellow acrylic paint. Let dry.
4. Glue on the frame tile.
5. Cover the edges with 1/2" border stickers.
6. Glue the photo to the tile.
7. Embellish the lower left corner of the base tile with a sticker.

Finish:
1. Seal the entire piece with two coats of thin-bodied glue. Let dry.
2. Pour on the two-part polymer coating. ◨

Bath Time

The Photo Display technique can be used with art prints as well as photos. This print is from a calendar.

Supplies

Paper: Calendar print, vintage motif decorative paper

Glue: Thin white glue

Foam Core Board: 1/2", 3/16"

Acrylic Craft Paint: Dark brown

Embellishments: Stickers of hot and cold taps, rub-on letters

Finish: 5 oz. two-part polymer coating

Tools: Brushes, art knife, cutting mat, ruler

How to

Base Tile:

1. Cut a 12" square from 1/2" foam core board.
2. Paint the edges with dark brown acrylic paint. Let dry.
3. Cover with vintage decorative paper.

Frame Tile:

1. Cut an 8-1/2" square from 3/16" foam core board.
2. Basecoat with dark brown acrylic paint. Let dry.
3. Glue to the base tile.

Picture Tile:

1. Cut a 7" square from 3/16" foam core board.
2. Paint the edges with dark brown acrylic paint.
3. Glue to the frame tile.
4. Cut the calendar print to fit.
5. Adhere to the picture tile.

Finish:

1. Embellish the base tile with stickers of hot and cold taps and rub-on letters.
2. Seal the entire piece with two coats of thin-bodied glue. Let dry.
3. Pour on the two-part polymer coating. ❖

Design
Mosaics

*Design Mosaics use the classic mosaic technique
of creating a design with pieces of color. Spaces left
between the pieces imitate the look of grout lines.
The project in this section uses cut paper pieces to
create the designs.*

Design Mosaics, Step by Step.

1. **Prepare.** Prepare the surface on which you will create the mosaic. See "Techniques for Surface Preparation."

2. **Cut.** Cut the decorative paper into the mosaic pieces. See "Cutting Tools & Techniques." Use a paper trimmer to cut a strip of paper, then cut the strips into smaller pieces with scissors. You can cut squares or rectangles or cut angled or three- or five-sided pieces. You can cut all the pieces at once since they won't be glued in sequence.

3. **Transfer the pattern.** Trace the pattern and transfer to the surface, using water-erase transfer paper. *Option:* Draw the pattern on the surface with a water- or air-erase pen.

4. **Glue.** Glue the paper mosaic pieces to the surface, using decoupage medium. See "Adhering Paper to Surfaces." Cut paper pieces into smaller pieces or curved pieces, if needed, to fit the design lines. Let dry.

5. **Seal.** If finishing with a polymer coating, seal the surface with two coats of thin-bodied white glue.

6. **Finish.** Apply clear varnish or a polymer coating. See "Protecting Your Project."

Plum Plate

The plate was first covered with a background of diamonds; the fruit design was glued on top. I used 12" x 12" sheets of decorative memory paper to create the design.

Continued on page 124

Plum Plate

continued from page 122

Supplies

Surface: Wooden plate, 10" diameter

Acrylic Craft Paints: Light green-gray, metallic gold (or colors that match your chosen papers)

Paper: Tan script, tan tapestry, green, dark red, plum, dark brown memory paper (preferably with a tapestry or decorative design)

Glue: Thin white glue

Finishes: Varnish crackle, dark brown antiquing medium, 4 oz. two-part polymer coating

Tools: Brushes, paper trimmer, scissors, sandpaper, sponge, water-erase pen or water-erase transfer paper

How to

Create the Background:

1. Basecoat the plate with light green-gray paint. Let dry.
2. Cut the tan script and tapestry papers into 2-1/2" x 4-1/4" diamonds. Decoupage them on the plate, alternating the two types. Let the excess paper extend over the rim of the plate. Let dry.
3. Use sandpaper to sand off the excess paper. (This gives the edge a perfect finish.)
4. Using a painting sponge, paint the rim of the plate with metallic gold paint. Let dry.
5. Apply crackle medium to the entire plate surface according to the package instructions.
6. Rub with brown antiquing to reveal cracks on the diamond paper pieces.

Add the Fruit Design:

1. Trace the plum branch pattern and transfer to the plate.
2. Cut the paper into pieces and fill in the pattern shapes, leaving small spaces between each piece to imitate the look of grout lines.

Finish:

1. Seal the plate with thin-bodied white glue. Let dry.
2. Apply a two-part polymer coating. ▪▪

Plum Plate Pattern

dark green

dark green

dark green

dark green

dark red

dark red

stem dark brown

Bonus Pattern
Use this to create your own project.

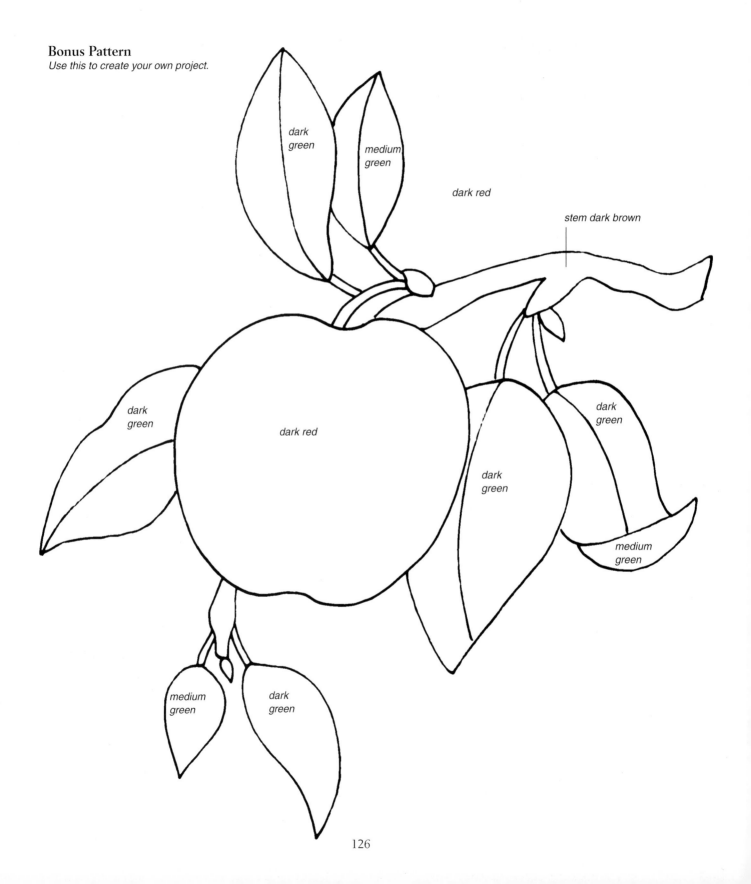

dark green

medium green

dark red

stem dark brown

dark green

dark red

dark green

dark green

medium green

medium green

dark green

Metric Conversion Chart

Inches to Millimeters and Centimeters

Inches	MM	CM	Inches	MM	CM
1/8	3	.3	2	51	5.1
1/4	6	.6	3	76	7.6
3/8	10	1.0	4	102	10.2
1/2	13	1.3	5	127	12.7
5/8	16	1.6	6	152	15.2
3/4	19	1.9	7	178	17.8
7/8	22	2.2	8	203	20.3
1	25	2.5	9	229	22.9
1-1/4	32	3.2	10	254	25.4
1-1/2	38	3.8	11	279	27.9
1-3/4	44	4.4	12	305	30.5

Yards to Meters

Yards	Meters	Yards	Meters
1/8	.11	3	2.74
1/4	.23	4	3.66
3/8	.34	5	4.57
1/2	.46	6	5.49
5/8	.57	7	6.40
3/4	.69	8	7.32
7/8	.80	9	8.23
1	.91	10	9.14
2	1.83		

Index